Iceland Travel guide 2024

Discover Iceland: A Traveler's Paradise

By : Dane Joe

Table of Contents

1. Introduction to Iceland: Land of Fire and Ice

- Brief overview of Iceland's geography, culture, and unique features.

Nestled in the North Atlantic Ocean, Iceland is a captivating land that seamlessly blends natural wonders with rich cultural heritage. This rough guide invites you to explore the essence of a country often referred to as the "Land of Fire and Ice," where geothermal wonders meet glaciers, and where folklore dances with the Northern Lights.

Geography and Climate:
Iceland's unique geographical makeup sets it apart. A realm shaped by volcanic activity, the country boasts otherworldly landscapes, from moss-covered lava fields to towering waterfalls. The juxtaposition of glaciers and hot springs creates an environment that is both rugged and ethereal. The Arctic climate adds to the allure, presenting travelers with an ever-changing canvas of weather, each season offering a distinct and breathtaking experience.

Cultural Tapestry:
Beyond its natural wonders, Iceland's cultural tapestry is woven with stories of Norse mythology, sagas, and a resilient spirit forged in the face of a challenging environment. Reykjavik, the world's northernmost capital, pulses with creativity and a

modern energy that coexists harmoniously with ancient traditions. Visitors will encounter a proud and warm community eager to share its heritage.

Landmarks that Define Iceland:
From the iconic Hallgrímskirkja church in Reykjavik to the mesmerizing Blue Lagoon and the thunderous Gullfoss waterfall along the Golden Circle, Iceland's landmarks are as diverse as they are breathtaking. This guide aims to unravel the stories behind these attractions and guide you through the hidden gems that dot the island, inviting you to witness the raw beauty that defines Iceland.

An Invitation to Adventure:
Whether you seek outdoor thrills like hiking on glaciers, bathing in geothermal springs, or chasing the elusive Northern Lights, Iceland extends an invitation to adventure-seekers and nature enthusiasts alike. Each fjord, volcano, and hot spring tells a tale, inviting you to be part of a narrative that unfolds with every step taken on this enchanting island.

Embark on a journey with this guide as your companion, unlocking the secrets of Iceland's landscapes, traditions, and the magical interplay between the elements that make this country truly extraordinary. Welcome to the beginning of an Icelandic adventure, where every moment promises a discovery and every landscape tells a story.

2. Getting Started: Your Gateway to Iceland

- Practical information on visas, currency, language, and transportation options.

Before you embark on your Icelandic adventure, it's essential to lay the groundwork for a seamless and enjoyable journey. This section serves as your comprehensive guide to the practicalities of visiting Iceland, ensuring that you are well-prepared for the wonders that await.

Visas and Entry Requirements:
Iceland, being a part of the Schengen Area, welcomes travelers from many countries without the need for a visa. However, it's crucial to check the specific entry requirements based on your nationality. Ensure that your passport is valid for the entirety of your stay and review any visa or permit conditions before boarding your flight to this Nordic paradise.

Currency and Banking:
The Icelandic Króna (ISK) is the official currency, and while credit cards are widely accepted, it's advisable to carry some cash, especially when venturing into more remote areas. Familiarize yourself with the currency exchange rates and locate ATMs in major towns for convenient access to Icelandic Króna.

Language and Communication:
Icelandic is the official language, but you'll find that English is widely spoken, making communication relatively straightforward for international travelers. Still, learning a few basic Icelandic phrases can enhance your experience and foster connections with locals who appreciate the effort.

Transportation:
Navigating Iceland is an integral part of the adventure. Whether you choose to rent a car, embark on guided tours, or utilize the well-connected bus system, understanding the transportation options is key. Consider the season of your visit – winter may require a four-wheel-drive vehicle for certain areas,

while summer opens up a network of roads and routes.

Weather Preparedness:
Iceland's weather is known for its unpredictability. Pack layers, waterproof clothing, and sturdy footwear, and be prepared for sudden changes. Checking the weather forecast regularly and adjusting your plans accordingly ensures a comfortable and safe exploration of the diverse landscapes.

Accommodation Booking:
From cozy guest houses to luxurious hotels and unique stays like traditional turf houses, Iceland offers a range of accommodation options. Booking in advance, especially during peak seasons, is advisable to secure your preferred lodging. This guide provides insights into various accommodations across the country, catering to different preferences and budgets.

By addressing these practical aspects, you set the stage for an immersive Icelandic experience. As you prepare to delve into the breathtaking landscapes and cultural richness, consider this section your gateway, ensuring that your journey is not only memorable but also hassle-free. Welcome to the enchanting world of Iceland – let the adventure begin!

3. Must-See Destinations: Unveiling Iceland's Spectacular Beauty

- Highlights of popular places like Reykjavik, Golden Circle, Blue Lagoon, and Jokulsarlon Glacier Lagoon.

Iceland is a land of astonishing contrasts and natural wonders, each destination offering a unique glimpse into the country's diverse beauty. In this section, we unravel the must-see destinations that define the Icelandic experience, guiding you through landscapes that range from geothermal marvels to glacial wonders.

Reykjavik: The Capital Marvel:

Begin your journey in Reykjavik, the beating heart of Iceland. This vibrant capital city seamlessly blends modern sophistication with a charming, small-town atmosphere. Explore the iconic Hallgrímskirkja church, stroll through the colorful streets of the Old Town, and immerse yourself in the lively arts and cultural scene. Reykjavik serves not only as a starting point but as a cultural hub that sets the tone for the rest of your Icelandic adventure.

The Golden Circle: A Tapestry of Wonders:

Embark on the Golden Circle, a route that encompasses three extraordinary natural phenomena. Start with the historic and geologically significant Thingvellir National Park, where the North American and Eurasian tectonic plates meet. Witness the explosive power of the Geysir geothermal area, home to the famous Strokkur geyser, and marvel at the majestic Gullfoss waterfall as it cascades into a rugged canyon. The Golden Circle presents a condensed showcase of Iceland's geological wonders.

Blue Lagoon: A Traspertery of Wonders:

Blue Lagoon, a geothermal spa surrounded by a
surreal lava field. The milky-blue waters, rich in
minerals, offer a unique and relaxing escape. Allow
the warm waters to envelop you as you take in the
otherworldly surroundings, creating memories that
linger long after you leave this enchanting oasis.

Jokulsarlon Glacier Lagoon: A Frozen Symphony:

Venture to the southeastern part of Iceland to discover the ethereal Jokulsarlon Glacier Lagoon. Marvel at the floating icebergs, calved from the nearby Vatnajokull Glacier, as they drift serenely in the lagoon. The juxtaposition of ice and water, framed by the surrounding mountains, creates a mesmerizing landscape that is both tranquil and awe-inspiring.

Skogafoss and Seljalandsfoss: Waterfall Wonders:

Iceland boasts a plethora of waterfalls, and two of the most captivating are Skogafoss and Seljalandsfoss. Skogafoss, with its powerful cascade, is a breathtaking sight, while Seljalandsfoss offers a unique experience as you can walk behind the curtain of water, providing a perspective like no other. These waterfalls epitomize the raw beauty of Iceland's natural wonders.

As you explore these must-see destinations, you'll find that each one contributes to the rich tapestry of Iceland's landscapes and cultural heritage. This section serves as your guide to unlocking the essence of these extraordinary places, inviting you to witness the magic that defines Iceland's allure.

4. Outdoor Adventures: Embracing Iceland's Elemental Beauty

- Information on hiking trails, hot springs, waterfalls, and opportunities for activities like glacier hiking and whale watching.

Iceland's untamed landscapes beckon adventurers to explore a realm shaped by fire, ice, and the relentless forces of nature. In this section, we delve into the outdoor wonders that define Iceland's rugged charm, inviting you to embark on exhilarating hikes, soak in geothermal springs, and witness nature's spectacular displays.

Landmannalaugar: Hiker's Paradise in the Highlands:

Venture into the colorful highlands of Iceland to discover Landmannalaugar, a geothermal oasis surrounded by rhyolite mountains. This area is a haven for hikers, offering a variety of trails that lead through surreal landscapes, hot springs, and obsidian lava fields. The Laugavegur Trail, starting from Landmannalaugar and winding through diverse terrains, stands as one of the world's most captivating trekking routes.

Þórsmörk: Valley of the Thunder God:

Nestled between glaciers, Þórsmörk (Thorsmork) is a
lush valley named after the Norse god Thor.
Accessible by special buses or 4x4 vehicles due to its
challenging terrain, Þórsmörk boasts hiking trails
that meander through birchwood forests, revealing
panoramic views of glaciers and volcanic landscapes.
It's a haven for nature lovers seeking solitude amid
awe-inspiring scenery.

Hot Springs and Geothermal Pools:

Iceland's geothermal activity manifests in numerous hot springs and pools, offering both relaxation and a chance to immerse yourself in the country's natural warmth. The Secret Lagoon in Flúðir, nestled in a geothermal area, and the less crowded Reykjadalur Hot Springs, reached by a scenic hike, provide intimate encounters with Iceland's geothermal wonders.

Glacier Hiking: Conquering the Ice Giants:

For an unforgettable adventure, don crampons and explore the icy realms of Vatnajokull, Europe's largest glacier. Guided glacier hikes allow you to navigate otherworldly ice formations, deep crevasses, and ice tunnels, providing a unique perspective on Iceland's frozen landscapes. Safety is paramount, and experienced guides ensure a thrilling yet secure glacial exploration.

Whale Watching: Maritime Encounters:

Iceland's rich marine ecosystem offers excellent opportunities for whale watching. Head to places like Húsavík, often referred to as the "Whale Watching Capital of Europe," for a chance to witness majestic cetaceans, including humpback whales, orcas, and minke whales, against the stunning backdrop of Iceland's northern coast.

Aurora Borealis: Chasing the Northern Lights:

Iceland's location near the Arctic Circle makes it a prime destination for witnessing the enchanting Aurora Borealis, or Northern Lights. The winter months, especially from September to March, offer optimal conditions for this celestial display. Journey to remote locations away from city lights for an unobstructed view of the dancing colors across the night sky.

Embark on these outdoor adventures, each offering a distinct encounter with Iceland's elemental beauty. Whether hiking through volcanic landscapes, soaking in hot springs, or marveling at glaciers, this section serves as your guide to embracing the untamed spirit of Iceland's natural wonders. Let the outdoors become your playground as you discover the diverse landscapes that make this island a haven for adventurous souls.

5. Cultural Experiences: Unveiling Iceland's Rich Heritage

- Recommendations for exploring Icelandic folklore, museums, and local traditions.

Beyond its breathtaking landscapes, Iceland's cultural tapestry is woven with sagas, folklore, and a vibrant contemporary spirit. In this section, we delve into the cultural experiences that define Iceland, inviting you to explore museums, connect with local traditions, and immerse yourself in a world where history and modernity coexist seamlessly.

National Museum of Iceland: A Journey Through Time:

Begin your cultural exploration in Reykjavik at the National Museum of Iceland. This institution traces the island's history from the Viking Age to the present day, showcasing artifacts, manuscripts, and exhibits that illuminate the nation's evolution. Dive into the sagas and stories that have shaped Iceland's identity and gain insights into the resilience of its people.

Árbær Open Air Museum: Preserving the Past:

Step back in time at the Árbær Open Air Museum, an immersive experience that transports visitors to rural Iceland in the 19th and 20th centuries. Authentic buildings, farmsteads, and artifacts depict daily life, providing a hands-on encounter with Iceland's agrarian heritage. Stroll through cobbled streets and engage with costumed guides to gain a deeper understanding of Iceland's cultural roots.

Icelandic Sagas: Literary Legacy:

The Icelandic sagas, epic narratives written in the Old Norse language, are a cornerstone of the country's literary heritage. Delve into these captivating tales of heroism, adventure, and mythology, which have been passed down through generations. Visit the Saga Museum in Reykjavik for a multimedia experience that brings these sagas to life, providing context to the stories etched into Iceland's cultural consciousness.

Traditional Icelandic Music and Dance:

Experience the soulful sounds of Icelandic music, rooted in centuries-old traditions. Attend local concerts or music festivals to immerse yourself in the haunting melodies of Icelandic folk music or contemporary works that draw inspiration from the country's landscapes. Additionally, explore traditional dance performances, such as the distinctive Icelandic ballads, showcasing the country's rich musical heritage.

Harpa Concert Hall: Architectural and Artistic Marvel:

In Reykjavik, the Harpa Concert Hall stands as a symbol of modern Icelandic architecture and a hub for cultural events. Admire its striking glass facade and explore the interior, where world-class performances, art exhibitions, and conferences unfold. The building itself is a testament to Iceland's commitment to fostering creativity and artistic expression.

Thorrablot: Culinary Tradition:

Partake in Thorrablot, an ancient Icelandic midwinter festival that celebrates traditional cuisine. Brave the culinary adventure as you sample unique dishes like fermented shark (hákarl) and sour sheep's head, accompanied by the strong spirit of Brennivín. Engaging in this feast is not just a culinary experience but a cultural immersion into Iceland's historic gastronomic traditions.

As you navigate through these cultural experiences, you'll discover the layers of Iceland's identity – a fusion of ancient sagas, modern creativity, and a profound connection to nature. This section serves as your guide to unraveling the cultural richness that defines Iceland, offering a deeper appreciation for the nation's history, art, and living traditions.

6. Wildlife and Nature: Exploring Iceland's Natural Abundance

- Insights into the diverse wildlife, birdwatching spots, and Iceland's commitment to environmental conservation.

Iceland's unique position at the confluence of geological forces and Arctic ecosystems creates a haven for diverse wildlife and awe-inspiring natural wonders. In this section, we embark on a journey through the country's pristine landscapes, encountering a rich array of flora and fauna that thrive in this land of fire and ice.

Birdwatching Havens:

Iceland is a paradise for birdwatchers, hosting an abundance of seabirds and migratory species. The cliffs of Látrabjarg in the Westfjords are home to one of the largest puffin colonies in the world. Witness these charming birds in their natural habitat, often perched on dramatic cliffs overlooking the North Atlantic. Additionally, explore the Jökulsárlón Glacier Lagoon, where birdlife harmonizes with the serene surroundings.

Arctic Foxes: The Furry Inhabitants:

The Arctic fox, Iceland's only native land mammal, is an elusive and resilient species that has adapted to the harsh Arctic conditions. Encounter these charming creatures in the wild, particularly in the remote Westfjords and Hornstrandir Nature Reserve. As Iceland's only mammalian land predator, the Arctic fox holds a special place in the country's ecological tapestry.

Marine Life: Whales and Seals:

Iceland's surrounding waters are teeming with marine life, making it an ideal destination for whale watching. Head to places like Húsavík, Akureyri, or the Snæfellsnes Peninsula for opportunities to spot humpback whales, orcas, minke whales, and blue whales. Coastal areas also offer a chance to observe seals basking on rocky shores, adding to the rich maritime experience.

Flora Amidst Fire and Ice:

Contrary to its name, Iceland boasts a surprising variety of flora, especially during the summer months. The vibrant lupine fields, moss-covered lava fields, and Arctic cotton grass create a colorful tapestry against the stark landscapes. Explore the Thorsmork Valley or the Hengill geothermal area to witness the resilience of Icelandic plants in the face of challenging conditions.

Conservation and Responsible Tourism:

Iceland places a strong emphasis on conservation and sustainable tourism practices. Learn about the country's commitment to preserving its unique ecosystems, from reforestation efforts to protecting fragile bird nesting areas. Embrace responsible tourism by staying on marked trails, respecting wildlife habitats, and supporting eco-friendly initiatives.

National Parks and Protected Areas:

Explore Iceland's national parks, such as Vatnajokull, Þingvellir, and Snæfellsjökull, each offering a distinct natural experience. From cascading waterfalls and glaciers to geothermal wonders, these protected areas showcase the diverse facets of Iceland's natural beauty. Follow designated trails to minimize environmental impact and immerse yourself in the pristine wilderness.

This section invites you to venture into the wild heart of Iceland, where nature's abundance unfolds in a captivating display. Whether you're captivated by birdwatching, fascinated by Arctic foxes, or drawn to the marine life surrounding the island, Iceland's wildlife and natural wonders await your exploration. As you tread lightly through these landscapes, you'll discover the delicate balance that makes Iceland a sanctuary for both wildlife and nature enthusiasts alike.

7. Seasonal Considerations: Navigating Iceland's Dynamic Weather and Events

- Tips for visiting in different seasons, including the unique experiences each season offers.

Iceland's ever-changing seasons play a pivotal role in shaping the country's landscapes and defining the character of your journey. In this section, we guide you through the nuances of each season, helping you tailor your visit to experience the unique charms and events that unfold throughout the year.

Summer: The Land of the Midnight Sun (May to August):

Summer in Iceland is a time of boundless daylight, with the sun barely setting on the horizon. This season unveils vibrant landscapes adorned with blooming wildflowers and cascading waterfalls. Explore the Highlands, embark on hiking trails, and witness the puffin colonies along coastal cliffs. Summer also brings an array of festivals, outdoor concerts, and events, making it an ideal time for cultural immersion.

Autumn: A Tapestry of Colors (September to November):

As autumn arrives, Iceland transforms into a canvas painted with hues of gold, red, and orange. Witness the magical dance of the Northern Lights as darkness gradually returns. Experience the annual sheep round-ups, where farmers gather their flocks from the Highlands, providing a glimpse into rural Icelandic traditions. Autumn offers a quieter atmosphere, ideal for those seeking serene landscapes and a touch of local authenticity.

Winter: Chasing the Northern Lights (December to February):

Winter enchants Iceland with its snow-covered landscapes and the mesmerizing dance of the Northern Lights. Head to remote locations away from city lights for optimal aurora viewing. Winter also presents opportunities for thrilling activities like ice cave exploration, snowmobiling on glaciers, and soaking in geothermal hot springs amidst the snowy surroundings. Despite the cold, the winter wonderland of Iceland is an invitation to witness the country's ethereal beauty.

Spring: Awakening Nature (March to April):

As winter retreats, Iceland experiences a gradual
thaw, unveiling a landscape awakening from its snowy
slumber. Spring is the time for birdwatching, with
migratory species returning to nest in the country's
diverse habitats. Witness the contrast of lingering
snow against budding vegetation and explore the
burgeoning energy of waterfalls and rivers. Spring is
an opportune season for those seeking a balance
between winter's tranquility and the vibrancy of
summer.

Festivals and Events:
Throughout the year, Iceland hosts a variety of
festivals celebrating music, art, literature, and local
traditions. The Reykjavik Arts Festival in summer,

Iceland Airwaves music festival in autumn, and the Winter Lights Festival in February are just a few examples. Attending these events provides a deeper connection to Iceland's cultural scene, offering a chance to celebrate with locals and fellow travelers.

Practical Considerations:
Regardless of the season, it's essential to pack accordingly. Layers, waterproof clothing, sturdy footwear, and accessories like hats and gloves are essential, especially in the colder months. Keep an eye on weather forecasts, road conditions, and daylight hours to plan your activities and travel safely.

Understanding the nuances of Iceland's seasons allows you to tailor your visit to match your preferences and interests. Whether you seek the endless daylight of summer, the magical Northern Lights of winter, or the colorful landscapes of autumn, each season in Iceland offers a distinct and unforgettable experience. As you embark on your journey, let the rhythm of the seasons guide you through the ever-changing beauty of this captivating island.

8. Local Cuisine: A Culinary Exploration of Authentic Icelandic Flavors

- Introduction to traditional Icelandic dishes and recommendations for local eateries.

Icelandic cuisine reflects the island's unique geography and cultural heritage, offering a culinary journey that combines traditional flavors with modern twists. In this section, we delve into the distinctive dishes and dining experiences that define Iceland's gastronomic landscape.

Fish and Seafood: The Bounty of the North Atlantic: Given its proximity to the North Atlantic Ocean, Iceland is renowned for its fresh and sustainable seafood. Try Icelandic fish staples like cod, haddock, and salmon, prepared in various ways such as grilled, smoked, or in hearty fish stews. Don't miss the opportunity to savor traditional dishes like "plokkfiskur," a comfort food made with fish, potatoes, onions, and béchamel sauce.

Lamb: A Taste of the Countryside:
Icelandic lamb, raised in the country's open landscapes, is a culinary delicacy known for its tender meat and unique flavor. "Hangikjöt," or smoked lamb, is a popular dish, especially during the festive season. It's often served with sweet peas, potatoes, and béchamel sauce, creating a harmonious blend of savory and sweet.

Skyr: Iceland's Dairy Delight:
Skyr, a traditional Icelandic dairy product, is a thick and creamy yogurt-like substance with a mild flavor. High in protein and low in fat, Skyr is often enjoyed with berries, honey, or as an ingredient in various desserts and smoothies. Embrace this local dairy delight as a healthy and tasty addition to your Icelandic culinary exploration.

Brennivín: The "Black Death" Schnapps:
Brennivín, often referred to as the "Black Death," is Iceland's signature schnapps. Distilled from fermented grain or potato mash and flavored with caraway seeds, it's a potent spirit with a distinctive taste. Embrace the local tradition by trying a shot of

Brennivín, often served during festive occasions and celebrations.

Hot Dogs and Street Food: An Icelandic Classic:
While it might seem simple, the Icelandic hot dog, or "pylsa," is a beloved national dish. Often enjoyed with crispy fried onions, raw onions, ketchup, sweet mustard, and remoulade, it's a quick and delicious snack that you'll find at hot dog stands throughout the country. Join the locals in savoring this iconic Icelandic street food.

Rúgbrauð and Flatkaka: Traditional Breads:
Explore Icelandic bread traditions with "rúgbrauð," a dense and sweet rye bread traditionally baked underground using geothermal heat. Pair it with local butter for a delightful treat. Additionally, try "flatkaka," a thin and soft unleavened bread often served with smoked fish or cured meats.

Culinary Adventures: Fine Dining and Farm-to-Table Experiences:
Reykjavik and other major towns offer a burgeoning culinary scene with restaurants that blend traditional Icelandic ingredients with contemporary techniques.

Explore farm-to-table dining experiences, where local produce and fresh ingredients are highlighted. Indulge in tasting menus that showcase the creativity of Icelandic chefs, offering a gastronomic journey through the country's flavors.

Embark on a culinary adventure in Iceland, where the flavors of the land and sea come together to create a unique and memorable dining experience. From traditional dishes rooted in centuries-old recipes to modern interpretations that reflect the vibrant energy of contemporary Icelandic cuisine, each bite tells a story of this enchanting island's culinary heritage.

9. Accommodation Options: Where to Stay in Iceland's Diverse Landscape

- Suggestions for hotels, guesthouses, and unique stays across the country.

Iceland's diverse landscapes are matched by a range of accommodation options that cater to every traveler's preferences, from cozy guesthouses to luxurious hotels and unique stays. In this section, we explore the different types of accommodations across the country, ensuring you find the perfect retreat for your Icelandic journey.

Hotels in Reykjavik: Urban Comfort with a Nordic Touch:
Reykjavik, Iceland's capital, boasts a variety of hotels ranging from boutique establishments to international chains. Experience urban comfort with Nordic design elements, often featuring sleek

interiors, panoramic views, and proximity to the city's cultural and culinary hotspots. Many hotels in Reykjavik also offer amenities like spas, fitness centers, and on-site dining options.

Guesthouses: Cozy Retreats with Local Flair:
For a more intimate and local experience, consider staying in a guesthouse. These family-run accommodations are scattered across Iceland, offering cozy rooms and personalized hospitality. Engage with locals, savor home-cooked meals, and gather around shared spaces for a genuine Icelandic experience. Guesthouses are prevalent in both urban and rural settings.

Farm Stays: Embracing Rural Iceland:
Immerse yourself in rural life by choosing a farm stay. Iceland's farms often open their doors to travelers, providing a unique opportunity to experience agricultural traditions and connect with the land. Wake up to stunning landscapes, participate in farm activities, and enjoy hearty home-cooked meals prepared with local ingredients.

Mountain Huts and Highland Cabins: Wilderness Retreats:
For those exploring Iceland's remote and rugged Highlands, mountain huts and cabins offer basic yet essential accommodations. These wilderness retreats provide shelter for hikers and nature enthusiasts traversing the challenging terrains. It's an opportunity to disconnect and immerse yourself in the untouched beauty of Iceland's interior.

Unique Stays: Sleeping in Extraordinary Settings:
Iceland offers a plethora of unique stays that elevate your lodging experience. Consider sleeping in a traditional turf house for a historic touch or booking a stay in a modern igloo for a futuristic twist. Remote cottages, treehouses, and even converted lighthouses provide unforgettable settings for your Icelandic adventure.

Luxury Lodges and Boutique Retreats: Indulgence in Nature:
Luxury lodges and boutique retreats cater to travelers seeking indulgence amidst Iceland's natural wonders. These high-end accommodations often blend seamlessly with the surrounding landscapes,

offering privacy, exclusive amenities, and personalized services. Relax in geothermal hot tubs, dine on gourmet cuisine, and unwind in style after a day of exploration.

Budget-Friendly Hostels: Affordable and Social:
For budget-conscious travelers and those seeking a social atmosphere, hostels provide affordable accommodation options. Iceland's hostels are well-equipped, with communal areas for mingling with fellow travelers. They are found in major towns and popular tourist destinations, offering a cost-effective way to experience the country.

Campgrounds and Camping Sites: Embracing Nature Directly:
Camping enthusiasts can take advantage of Iceland's numerous campgrounds and designated camping sites. Whether you're in a tent, camper, or motorhome, camping allows you to be immersed in nature, with many sites offering basic facilities and stunning views.

Choosing the right accommodation depends on your travel style, preferences, and the regions you plan to explore. Whether you opt for the comfort of urban hotels, the charm of guesthouses, the serenity of farm stays, or the adventure of camping in the wild, Iceland's diverse accommodation options ensure a memorable and personalized stay in this captivating land.

10. Practical Tips: Navigating Iceland with Ease and Enjoyment

- Packing advice, safety tips, and other practical information for a smooth trip.

Embarking on a journey to Iceland requires thoughtful planning and an understanding of the practicalities that come with exploring this unique destination. In this section, we delve into a comprehensive set of practical tips to ensure your trip is smooth, enjoyable, and filled with unforgettable experiences.

1. Packing Essentials:
   - Pack layers: Iceland's weather can be unpredictable, so having layers allows you to adapt to changing conditions.

- Waterproof clothing: Invest in quality waterproof gear, including a sturdy rain jacket and waterproof pants.

- Sturdy footwear: Comfortable, waterproof boots are essential, especially for outdoor activities like hiking.

- Accessories: Don't forget essentials like a hat, gloves, and a good-quality backpack for day trips.

2. Safety First:

- Respect local guidelines: Follow safety guidelines, especially when venturing into natural areas or participating in activities like glacier hiking.

- Inform someone of your plans: If exploring remote areas, let someone know your itinerary and expected return time.

- Emergency numbers: Familiarize yourself with emergency contact numbers and local services.

3. Currency and Payment:

- Icelandic Króna (ISK): While credit cards are widely accepted, having some local currency is advisable, especially in more remote areas.

- ATMs: Locate ATMs in major towns for convenient currency exchange.

4. Language:

- English is widely spoken, but learning a few basic Icelandic phrases can enhance your experience and show respect for the local culture.

5. Transportation:

- Renting a car: If exploring beyond major cities, renting a car provides flexibility and access to remote areas.
- Public transportation: Buses operate between towns, but schedules may be limited, especially in more remote regions.

6. Weather Awareness:

- Check the weather forecast regularly, especially if engaging in outdoor activities. Iceland's weather can change rapidly.

7. Daylight Variations:

- Be aware of daylight variations: In summer, Iceland experiences almost continuous daylight, while winter sees shorter days. Plan activities accordingly.

8. Respect Nature and Wildlife:

- Stay on marked trails: Respect environmental conservation efforts by sticking to designated paths.
- Wildlife observation: Keep a safe distance from animals, especially nesting birds and seals.

9. Wi-Fi and Connectivity:
- Most accommodations, cafes, and tourist information centers offer Wi-Fi, but connectivity may be limited in remote areas.

10. Culinary Adventures:
- Try local dishes: Explore Icelandic cuisine, from traditional lamb dishes to unique treats like fermented shark. Embrace the culinary adventure.

11. Photography Tips:
- Capture the magic: Iceland's landscapes offer stunning photo opportunities. Ensure your camera equipment is suitable for various conditions.

12. Pre-Booking Activities:
- For popular activities like glacier tours or Northern Lights excursions, consider pre-booking to secure your spot.

13. Health Considerations:

   - Carry any necessary medications and have travel insurance that covers medical emergencies.

14. Local Customs:

   - Familiarize yourself with local customs and be mindful of cultural sensitivities.

By incorporating these practical tips into your travel preparations, you'll be well-equipped to navigate Iceland's dynamic environment and make the most of your journey. Whether chasing waterfalls, exploring geothermal wonders, or marveling at the Northern Lights, these tips ensure that your Icelandic adventure is not only memorable but also filled with ease and enjoyment.

Road Trip Adventures: Exploring Iceland's Scenic Routes

Embarking on a road trip in Iceland is a thrilling adventure that allows you to immerse yourself in the country's stunning landscapes at your own pace. In this section, we'll guide you through some of the most iconic and scenic routes, ensuring your road trip becomes a journey of discovery and awe.

1. The Ring Road (Route 1):
   - Overview: The Ring Road is Iceland's main highway, encircling the entire island and offering a comprehensive tour of its diverse landscapes.
   - Highlights:
   - Golden Circle: A detour from the Ring Road, featuring Thingvellir National Park, Geysir geothermal area, and Gullfoss waterfall.
   - Vatnajokull National Park: Home to Europe's largest glacier, with opportunities for glacier hikes and ice cave explorations.
   - East Fjords: Scenic coastal landscapes, charming fishing villages, and birdwatching opportunities.

2. Snæfellsnes Peninsula:
   - Overview: Often referred to as "Iceland in Miniature," this peninsula is a microcosm of the country's diverse geography.
   - Highlights:
   - Snæfellsjokull National Park: A captivating area surrounding the iconic Snæfellsjokull glacier-volcano.

- Kirkjufell: An iconic mountain often photographed with the nearby Kirkjufellsfoss waterfall.
- Arnarstapi and Hellnar: Charming coastal villages with unique rock formations and bird cliffs.

3. The Westfjords:
- Overview: A remote and less-traveled region, the Westfjords offer dramatic fjords, towering cliffs, and rich birdlife.
- Highlights:
- Dynjandi Waterfall: A series of cascading waterfalls surrounded by pristine wilderness.
- Látrabjarg Cliffs: Europe's westernmost point, home to puffin colonies and stunning sea cliffs.
- Isafjordur: The largest town in the Westfjords, known for its historic charm and cultural events.

4. The South Coast:
- Overview: A mesmerizing stretch of coastline with black sand beaches, glaciers, and powerful waterfalls.
- Highlights:

- Seljalandsfoss and Skogafoss: Two iconic waterfalls with unique features, including the ability to walk behind Seljalandsfoss.
- Vik: A picturesque village with the famous Reynisfjara Black Sand Beach and basalt sea stacks.
- Jokulsarlon Glacier Lagoon: A glacial lagoon dotted with icebergs, offering boat tours and a stunning view of Vatnajokull Glacier.

5. The Highlands:
- Overview: A rugged and remote interior region accessible during the summer months, providing a true off-the-beaten-path experience.
- Highlights:
- Landmannalaugar: A geothermal oasis surrounded by colorful mountains, popular for hiking and hot springs.
- Askja Caldera: A volcanic caldera with a striking blue lake, accessible via a challenging gravel road.
- Kerlingarfjoll: A mountain range featuring geothermal areas and vibrant rhyolite mountains.

6. The Diamond Circle:

- Overview: Located in the north, the Diamond Circle showcases a collection of natural wonders and geological marvels.
    - Highlights:
    - Húsavík: Known as the "Whale Watching Capital of Europe," offering whale watching tours.
    - Dettifoss: Europe's most powerful waterfall, thundering over a basalt canyon.
    - Asbyrgi Canyon: A horseshoe-shaped canyon surrounded by lush vegetation and walking trails.

7. F-Roads and Highlands Exploration:
    - Overview: F-Roads are gravel roads that lead to the Highlands, offering access to some of Iceland's most remote and untouched landscapes.
    - Highlights:
    - Fjallabak Nature Reserve: A wilderness area with volcanic landscapes, hot springs, and the famous Laugavegur hiking trail.
    - Langjokull Ice Cave: A man-made ice cave within Langjokull Glacier, accessible by a guided tour.

8. Practical Road Trip Tips:

- Car Rental: Choose a suitable vehicle, considering the terrain you plan to cover. Four-wheel-drive (4WD) vehicles are recommended for F-Roads.

- Fuel Stations: Plan your refueling stops, especially in remote areas where fuel stations may be scarce.

- Accommodations: Book accommodations in advance, especially during the peak summer season.

- Road Conditions: Check road conditions regularly, especially in winter when some roads may be impassable.

Embark on your road trip adventure, where each turn reveals a new facet of Iceland's breathtaking beauty. Whether you choose the well-traveled Ring Road or venture into the remote Highlands, the journey itself becomes an integral part of the Icelandic experience, inviting you to explore, discover, and connect with the land of fire and ice.

11. Useful Phrases for Traveling in Iceland

- Basic Icelandic phrases to help travelers communicate.

Traveling to a foreign country becomes more enriching and enjoyable when you can communicate with the locals using their language. While English is widely spoken in Iceland, learning some basic Icelandic phrases can enhance your experience and demonstrate respect for the local culture. Here's a comprehensive list of useful phrases to help you navigate your journey:

1. Greetings and Basic Phrases:
   - Hello: Halló
   - Good morning: Góðan morgun
   - Good afternoon: Góðan dag
   - Good evening: Gott kvöld
   - Goodbye: Bless
   - Please: Vinsamlegast
   - Thank you: Takk

- Yes: Já
- No: Nei
- Excuse me: Afsakið

2. Basic Questions:
   - How are you?: Hvernig hefurðu það?
   - What is your name?: Hvað heitir þú?
   - My name is...: Ég heiti...
   - Where are you from?: Hvaðan ert þú?
   - I'm from...: Ég er frá...

3. Navigating and Directions:
   - Where is...?: Hvar er...?
   - How do I get to...?: Hvernig kem ég til...?
   - Left: Vinstri
   - Right: Hægri
   - Straight ahead: Beint fram

4. Dining and Food:
   - I would like...: Ég ætla að fá...
   - Water: Vatn
   - Coffee: Kaffi
   - Beer: Bjór
   - Cheers!: Skál!
   - The bill, please: Reikninginn, takk

5. Accommodations and Reservations:

- Do you have any rooms available?: Eru laus herbergi?
- I have a reservation: Ég hef bókun
- Check-in/check-out: Innritun/útritun

6. Emergencies and Safety:

- Help!: Hjálp!
- I need a doctor: Ég þarf læknishjálp
- Where is the nearest hospital?: Hvar er næsta sjúkrahús?
- I've lost my...: Ég hef tapað...

7. Cultural Interactions:

- I don't understand: Ég skil ekki
- Can you speak more slowly?: Gætirðu talað hægar?
- What does this mean?: Hvað þýðir þetta?
- I'm learning Icelandic: Ég er að læra íslensku

8. Expressing Gratitude and Apologies:

- I'm sorry: Mér þykir leitt
- Excuse me (to get attention): Afsakið
- Thank you very much: Mikill þakkir

- You're welcome: Verði þér að góðu

9. Making Friends and Socializing:
   - Can we be friends?: Getum við orðið vinir?
   - What do you like to do for fun?: Hvaða skemmtun líkar þér við?
   - Let's hang out!: Höngum saman!
   - Do you want to go for a drink?: Viltu fara á drykk?

Learning these phrases will not only facilitate practical interactions but also foster connections with the Icelandic people. Embrace the opportunity to engage with the local culture, and your journey through Iceland will be enriched with meaningful encounters, shared experiences, and heartfelt moments.

12. Maps and Itineraries

- Sample itineraries for varying trip durations and maps for navigating key areas.

Navigation Essentials: Maps and Itineraries for Exploring Iceland

When embarking on a journey through Iceland's diverse landscapes, having well-prepared maps and itineraries is crucial for a smooth and enjoyable adventure. In this section, we delve into the importance of detailed maps and thoughtfully crafted itineraries to guide you through the wonders of the land of fire and ice.

1. Comprehensive Maps:
   - Road Maps: Obtain detailed road maps that cover the entirety of Iceland, including the Ring Road (Route 1) and F-Roads if you plan to venture into the Highlands. These maps should highlight key landmarks, attractions, and accommodations.

   - Topographic Maps: For hiking enthusiasts and those exploring off-the-beaten-path areas, topographic maps provide valuable information about elevation, terrain, and trails. This is especially crucial in the Highlands, where the landscape can be challenging.

   - Digital Maps: Utilize digital mapping applications or GPS devices for real-time navigation. Ensure these tools are accessible offline, as some remote areas may lack internet connectivity. Popular mapping apps include Google Maps, Maps.me, and dedicated GPS devices like Garmin.

   - Tourist Information Centers: Visit local tourist information centers to obtain updated maps, brochures, and personalized advice. These centers often provide insights into road conditions, weather forecasts, and noteworthy attractions.

2. Itinerary Planning:
   - Define Your Interests: Tailor your itinerary based on your interests, whether it's exploring waterfalls, geothermal areas, historical sites, or engaging in outdoor activities. Iceland offers a myriad of experiences, so identifying your

preferences will help you craft a well-rounded itinerary.

- Consider Seasonal Factors: Iceland's seasons significantly impact the accessibility of certain areas and the activities available. For example, summer offers endless daylight for exploration, while winter showcases the magical Northern Lights. Plan activities and routes accordingly.

- Accommodation Reservations: Secure accommodations in advance, especially during peak seasons. Your itinerary should include details such as check-in/check-out dates, locations, and contact information for each lodging. This ensures a comfortable and stress-free stay.

- Flexibility: While it's crucial to have a well-defined itinerary, allow for flexibility. Weather conditions, unexpected discoveries, or the desire to linger in a particular area may prompt changes to your schedule. Embrace spontaneity for a more authentic experience.

- Time Management: Be mindful of travel times between destinations, considering road conditions and potential stops. Allocate sufficient time for each activity, whether it's exploring a national park, hiking a trail, or enjoying a local festival.

3. Safety Considerations:
   - Emergency Contacts: Include emergency contact numbers, including the Icelandic emergency services hotline (112), in your itinerary. Familiarize yourself with the location of hospitals, police stations, and other essential services along your route.

   - Weather Updates: Regularly check weather forecasts, especially if you plan outdoor activities. Iceland's weather can change rapidly, and being informed allows you to make safe and informed decisions.

   - Road Conditions: Stay informed about road conditions, especially if you're traveling in winter or venturing into the Highlands. The Icelandic Road and Coastal Administration (Vegagerðin) provides real-time updates on road conditions.

- Leave No Trace Principles: Emphasize responsible tourism by adhering to "Leave No Trace" principles. Respect natural habitats, follow marked trails, and dispose of waste responsibly.

4. Cultural Experiences:
    - Local Events and Festivals: Integrate local events and festivals into your itinerary to immerse yourself in Iceland's culture. Check for celebrations, music festivals, and cultural gatherings happening during your visit.

    - Museum and Gallery Visits: Explore Iceland's rich cultural heritage by including visits to museums and galleries in your itinerary. Learn about the country's history, art, and traditions to deepen your appreciation for its uniqueness.

    - Culinary Exploration: Plan stops at local eateries, especially those offering traditional Icelandic cuisine. Trying local dishes adds a flavorful dimension to your journey, and each region may have its culinary specialties.

Crafting a well-balanced itinerary, coupled with detailed maps, ensures that your exploration of Iceland is not only efficient but also enriching. Whether you're captivated by the geological wonders, cultural experiences, or outdoor adventures, a thoughtfully prepared plan becomes the compass guiding you through the captivating landscapes of this extraordinary destination.

13. Capturing Iceland's Beauty: In-Depth Photography Tips for Every Adventurer

- Guidance on capturing the stunning landscapes and natural beauty of Iceland.

Iceland's otherworldly landscapes provide a breathtaking canvas for photographers, from majestic waterfalls to rugged mountains and the elusive Northern Lights. In this comprehensive guide, we delve into photography tips to help you capture the essence of Iceland's beauty, ensuring your images reflect the magic of this extraordinary land.

1. Chasing the Light:
   - Golden Hour Magic: Take advantage of Iceland's extended golden hour, especially during summer when the sun barely sets. The soft, warm light enhances landscapes and creates a magical atmosphere. Aim to shoot during sunrise or sunset for optimal results.

- Aurora Hunting: If your journey aligns with the Northern Lights season (September to April), plan night shoots in locations away from light pollution. Check aurora forecasts and be patient, as clear, dark skies increase your chances of witnessing and photographing the auroras.

2. Equipment Essentials:
   - Sturdy Tripod: Iceland's diverse terrains may require long exposure shots. A sturdy tripod is essential for capturing sharp images, especially during low-light conditions.

   - Wide-Angle Lens: Invest in a wide-angle lens to capture the vastness of Iceland's landscapes. It's ideal for shooting waterfalls, glaciers, and expansive vistas. Consider lenses with low aperture values for better performance in low light.

   - Telephoto Lens: Bring a telephoto lens for wildlife and bird photography, allowing you to capture distant subjects while maintaining image quality.

   - Camera Protection: Iceland's weather can be unpredictable. Carry weather-sealed camera gear and use rain covers to protect your equipment from rain and spray, especially when shooting near waterfalls.

3. Composition Techniques:
   - Foreground Elements: Incorporate interesting foreground elements to add depth to your compositions. Rocks, plants, or ice formations can serve as compelling anchors.

   - Leading Lines: Utilize natural lines, such as rivers, roads, or rock formations, to guide the viewer's eye through the image and create a sense of movement.

   - Rule of Thirds: Apply the rule of thirds to compose visually appealing images. Place key elements along the grid lines or at intersections to create a balanced and dynamic composition.

   - Framing: Use natural elements like arches or overhanging branches to frame your subject, drawing attention to the focal point of your photograph.

4. Mastering Long Exposures:
   - Smooth Water Effect: Capture the ethereal beauty of Iceland's waterfalls by using long exposure

to create silky, flowing water. A neutral density (ND) filter is essential to achieve longer shutter speeds in bright conditions.

- Aurora Trails: Experiment with long exposures during Northern Lights displays to capture vibrant aurora trails across the night sky. A wide aperture and high ISO settings help capture more light.

- Cloud Movement: Embrace the dynamic nature of Iceland's skies by incorporating cloud movement into your images. Use long exposures to create a sense of motion in the clouds.

5. Weather Preparedness:
   - Layered Clothing: Dress in layers to stay comfortable in Iceland's changing weather. This allows you to focus on photography without being hindered by the elements.

- Lens Cleaning Kit: Iceland's mist and rain can lead to lens condensation. Carry a lens cleaning kit to ensure your images remain clear and sharp.

- Weather Apps: Stay updated on weather conditions using reliable apps. Understanding the forecast helps plan your shoots and adapt to changing conditions.

6. Exploring Unique Perspectives:
- Drone Photography: Capture aerial perspectives of Iceland's landscapes using a drone. Ensure you are aware of and adhere to local regulations for drone usage.

- Low-Level Shots: Get close to the ground to capture unique angles. Iceland's moss-covered lava fields and vibrant flora provide excellent opportunities for low-level shots.

- Underwater Photography: If you have the equipment and expertise, explore underwater photography in locations like Silfra Fissure, where crystal-clear waters reveal a mesmerizing underwater world.

7. Post-Processing Techniques:

- RAW Format: Shoot in RAW to retain maximum information in your images, allowing for more flexibility during post-processing.

- Editing Software: Learn and utilize post-processing tools like Adobe Lightroom or Capture One to enhance your images. Adjust exposure, contrast, and color balance to bring out the best in your photographs.

- HDR Imaging: Experiment with High Dynamic Range (HDR) techniques to capture a wider range of tones in challenging lighting conditions. Blend multiple exposures for a balanced and detailed result.

Embarking on a photographic journey through Iceland requires a blend of technical proficiency, creativity, and adaptability to the unique conditions of this remarkable destination. Whether you're capturing the dance of the Northern Lights or the raw power of a waterfall, these photography tips aim to elevate your skills and ensure that your visual storytelling reflects the awe-inspiring beauty of Iceland.

14. Comprehensive Travel Resources for an Icelandic Adventure

- Recommendations for useful websites, apps, and local services.

Embarking on an Icelandic adventure requires careful planning and access to reliable travel resources. In this detailed guide, we explore a wide range of travel resources that will help you navigate everything from itinerary planning to cultural immersion, ensuring a seamless and enriching journey through the land of fire and ice.

1. Official Tourism Websites:

   - Visit Iceland: The official tourism website of Iceland, Visit Iceland, provides a wealth of information on attractions, activities, accommodations, and practical travel tips. Explore their detailed guides and interactive maps to plan your itinerary effectively.

- Icelandic Road and Coastal Administration (Vegagerðin): Stay informed about road conditions, closures, and real-time updates by checking Vegagerðin's website. This is especially crucial for those venturing into the Highlands, where road conditions can change rapidly.

2. Accommodation Booking Platforms:
   - Booking.com, Airbnb, and Hotels.com: These platforms offer a wide range of accommodations, from hotels and guesthouses to unique stays like cabins and farmhouses. Read reviews, compare prices, and book in advance, especially during peak travel seasons.

   - Hostelworld: Ideal for budget-conscious travelers, Hostelworld provides a vast selection of hostels in various locations across Iceland. It's a valuable resource for those seeking affordable and social accommodation options.

3. Transportation Services:
   - Rental Car Companies: Major rental car companies such as Hertz, Avis, and Europcar operate in Iceland. Renting a car provides flexibility, especially if you

plan to explore beyond major cities. Ensure your vehicle is suitable for Icelandic roads, including F-Roads if applicable.

- Public Transportation: Strætó is Iceland's public transportation system, offering bus services between towns. While not as extensive as in some other countries, it's a viable option for those without a car. Plan your routes and check schedules in advance.

4. Weather and Natural Phenomena:
   - Icelandic Meteorological Office: Stay informed about weather conditions, forecasts, and alerts by visiting the Icelandic Meteorological Office's website. This is crucial, especially for outdoor activities and Northern Lights viewing.

- Aurora Forecast Websites: Track the likelihood of witnessing the Northern Lights by using dedicated aurora forecast websites such as the Space Weather Prediction Center or the Aurora Service Europe.

5. Cultural and Event Information:

- Icelandic National Broadcasting Service (RÚV): Stay updated on local news, events, and cultural programs by visiting RÚV's website. It provides insights into Icelandic culture, current affairs, and upcoming events.

- Local Event Calendars: Explore local event calendars for festivals, concerts, and cultural gatherings. Websites like Guide to Iceland or local town websites often feature event listings.

6. Safety and Emergency Contacts:
- 112 Iceland App: Download the 112 Iceland app, which provides a direct connection to emergency services. It also includes your GPS coordinates, allowing quick response in case of emergencies.

- Icelandic Association for Search and Rescue (ICE-SAR): Familiarize yourself with ICE-SAR's website, which provides essential safety information, including guidelines for outdoor activities and emergency procedures.

7. Travel Forums and Blogs:

- Reddit's Iceland Travel Community: Engage with fellow travelers, ask questions, and share experiences on Reddit's Iceland travel community. It's a valuable platform for gaining insights and real-time advice.

- Travel Blogs and YouTube Channels: Explore travel blogs and YouTube channels dedicated to Iceland. Personal narratives, tips, and visual guides can provide valuable perspectives and inspiration for your journey.

8. Language Learning Resources:
- Icelandic Online: Familiarize yourself with basic Icelandic phrases using resources like Icelandic Online. While English is widely spoken, learning a few local phrases enhances your cultural experience.

- Language Apps: Language learning apps like Duolingo or Babbel often include Icelandic modules, offering a convenient way to pick up some language skills before your trip.

9. Local Guides and Tours:

- Local Tour Operators: Research and book tours with reputable local operators. Whether it's a glacier hike, whale watching, or a Golden Circle tour, local guides enhance your experience and provide insights into Iceland's natural wonders.

- I Heart Reykjavik Blog: Run by a local guide, the I Heart Reykjavik blog offers valuable insights into planning your Reykjavik visit and beyond, including self-drive itineraries and tips.

10. Photography and Navigation Apps:
   - Photography Apps: Apps like PhotoPills or The Photographer's Ephemeris help plan photo shoots, including sunrise and sunset times, moon phases, and celestial events.

   - Navigation Apps: Reliable navigation apps such as Google Maps, Maps.me, or Waze are useful for driving routes, especially when exploring less-traveled areas.

By leveraging these comprehensive travel resources, you'll be equipped with the knowledge and tools to make the most of your Icelandic adventure. Whether you're a nature enthusiast, cultural explorer, or seeking thrilling outdoor activities, these resources serve as valuable companions, ensuring a memorable and well-prepared journey through the captivating landscapes of Iceland.

Remember to adapt the guide based on the specific needs and interests of your audience!

Printed in Great Britain
by Amazon

37634999R00056